FAIRY GIRLS
2
MANGA BY BOKU
BASED ON A STORY BY HIRO MASHIMA

CONTENTS

Chapter 6:
Fairies Love Resorts?!

AFTER THE GRAND MAGIC GAMES...
...THE REPUTATION OF FAIRY TAIL ROSE AND OUR USUAL SPIRIT WAS RESTORED.
BUT...
...WHEN I SEE STUFF LIKE THIS, IT MAKES MY STOMACH CHURN.
DESTRUCTION OF CASTLE PROPERTY
ATTEMPTED KID-NAPPING OF KING
FOUR-WOMAN TEAM
REWARD: 1,500,000 JEWELS
W-?!
BAM
What is this?!
Why are we wanted criminals?
Wait, we don't even look like that!
But if we did, we'd be in real trouble, Lucy-san!
But we were the ones who saved the kingdom and the King!
And this is how they thank us?!
Heh heh...
SHK

So all of you *were* behind the crime!
For pity's sake!
Eeek!!
F-First Master?!
Hi there!
You too, Carla?!
C-Crime...? What are you talking about?
You can't fool me!
I have some idea of what my guild members are all up to.

Still, I never suspected Fairy Tail would be behind such a massive crisis.
RUMBLE
RUMBLE
RUMBLE
Eeeek!
GRIN
And you did wonderfully.
...
Huh?
Wait, did you just say...
I wish you wouldn't look so guilty.

Isn't it only natural to be praised when you save a kingdom?
And I've reserved a small gift for anyone who does such deeds!
It's an all-expenses-paid vacation to a resort!

What?
Excuse me?

What?!

VWAAM

It's a resort town on the waters of the southern seas!
I went ahead and made the reservations.
Thank you, Carla !!
Set your troubles aside and go have some fun! At least for today!
But is this all right? Four members skipping out while the rest of the guild is so busy?
ZSHHH
Makarov was kind enough to give permission, and all it took was one tantrum!
He's such a sweet child!
FLAIL FLAIL
Four of our top members at a time like this?!
I want us all to go!
Isn't this an abuse of power ?!
TUMP TUMP TUMP
You know, if we headed back now...
True! After all, Gray-sama is nowhere around.
Wait just one moment !!
Eee!
ZOOM

If I may– I am Gen, manager of our humble resort.
And I'm Lilly, an em-ployee here.
After a guest travels such a long way to get here, we cannot stand by and watch them return home!
ROAR
I'll be honest... We're troubled because we can't attract guests!
So please let us wait on you hand and foot!
FWOOH
What should Juvia do?
No one has ever come on to her so aggressively before.
Me neither.
Of course! We'd *love* to stay here!
First Master ?!
Oh, can't we?
Urk! U-Um, well...
SPARKLE

If it is the wish of the first master...
...we can endure a day.
Erza?
WHISPER
WHISPER
Are you sure?
Even the first master was once a regular little girl.
And yet, was she able to make lasting memories? To revel in the fruits of youth? I doubt it.
...Ah!
Well, when you put it that way...
...
Personally, I'd like to have a nice long talk with the first master!
Very well... Today, we'll go and live it up!
Yay!
Y-You have our gratitude! Now please enjoy your stay!
SMIRK
Yes...
Enjoy it, while you can...

Here it comes!
There!
TMP
All right!

Ahh...
It's been too long since I did this!

And if that day arrives and the world comes crashing down...
...it will be the wizards who trigger it.
So true.
Ma'am?
You can?
SPLECH

You can live to provide us sustenance.
?!
GRAB
You naive wizard!
Huh?
When did this happen?
GRAB
!!
What is this?!
It's like my strength is being drained away...
ZLURP
ZLURP
ZLURP
ZLURP
M-miss ...?
Ha ha ha!
18
Things?
happened lately...
There were tons of strange occurrences. Some were more obvious than others.
LIKE THAT GUY...
Yes...
I suppose so.
AND THIS GUY...
16

BOOM
?!
Urn...
Kh!
ズズズ
ZLURP
You guys!
I don't think they'll be moving anytime soon.
After all, they drank a full dose of my guild's special sleeping medicine.
Unlike you.
Huh?!
P- Please, tell me this is just some stunt...
Pft!

DWOOM
Does it *look* like one to you?!
Uwaah!
VWOOM
Aaah!
GRASH
Ow...
What is this ...?
A hidden side of the resort?
...
Huh?!

BOOM

Heh heh...
I just love a pretty, sandy beach...
ZZZLURP
Beaches are the best!
Best resort ever!
ZLURP
ZLURP
?!
These people ...
They're under illusions!
WHOOSH
Provided by the magic-absorbing machine that we developed!
We are Ant Lion!
We pretend to be a resort, but we're a dark guild that feeds on wizards' magical powers!
Magic-absorbing machine?
Feeds on...?
It's exactly what it sounds like–a device that sucks up a wizard's magical power.
Those tentacles suck out magic...
ZZLURP
!

That way, they don't put up a fight.
And in exchange, it leaves them with the illusion of spending a blissful time at a resort!
So...
...what they're seeing now...
All an illusion.
Well, except for the sea and beach.
FWOOOHH
...!
GRIMP
Ugh...
SLIP
We gather up the magic and sell it on the black market.
A pretty sweet deal, if you ask me.
Better than worrying about future prospects!

ZLURP
Aah!
So just sit back, relax, and enjoy our resort... **forever!**
You're just food for our guild!
ZLURP
ZLURP
ZLURP

ZLURP
ZLURP
Kh...
This is bad!
Is it the illusion ...?
But this might not be so bad...
They've got loads of other wizards, too, right?
They probably needed a vacation!
I'm no differ-ent...
It might be nice to forget it all and stay here...
WAVER
WAVER
SST

THUMP
But, you're different from the other wizards, see?
Be-cause ...
...You're a Fairy Tail wizard!
?
カプッ
CHOMP

Open!
Gate of the Lion Palace!
She had a key...
...in her cleavage?!

Eyaah!
DOKAAM

That was a close call!
If I hadn't kept a key there just in case the unthinkable happened...
...this could've been really bad!
HUFF HUFF
Impos-sible!
How?!
ZOOOOSH
The illusion was perfect!
Nobody's ever broken it before!
True, it was such a perfect resort, I couldn't have believed it was an illusion.
A place I wouldn't mind living in!
But...
It's still just a resort!
It's only fun to visit! Not to live in!
BOOM
Spending every day of your life in a resort is kind of hard to believe... and weird, too.
GONG
Really?
Dam-mit!
If that's the case...
VWAH

...We'll gather up the magic from all the wizards we've assembled so far...
...and crush you with it!
No, you...
... won't!
BOOM

Huh?
No way!
That's the magic of nearly 100 people...

REGULUS
IMPACT!

ZWAAMM

DOGOOM
Im...
Impossi-
ble...
Phew!
You
know
what...
...Fairy
Tail is
way more
fun than
any resort!
Sigh
...
So
in the
end...

...you had predict-ed...
...just about everything that happened at the resort?
Tee hee hee! Sorry about that!
I just hap-pened to hear a rumor...
...but it wasn't an official job, and I couldn't personally help out.
Th- That's true...
But ***before all that,*** it was pretty fun, wasn't it?
Huh?
And look how smooth your skin is!
GLEEM
GLEEM
Urk!
It *is* true.

It seems that their massage abilities weren't a lie.
A talent gone to waste...
But I guess you couldn't really call that a vacation.

So this time, I'm taking you to a *real* resort!
How about tomorrow?
W-we don't want to resort to that.
At least for a while, anyway.

AND A LITTLE LATER ...
...IT WAS REPORTED THAT THE SAME FOUR CRIMINALS ATTACKED A BEACH RESORT.
AND THE REWARD FOR THEIR CAPTURE WENT UP EVEN MORE.
2000000J
BOOM
No way!

Chapter 7: Is This...a First for Wendy?!

OVE RESEARCH CLUB

KENDO CLUB

FAIRY GIRLS

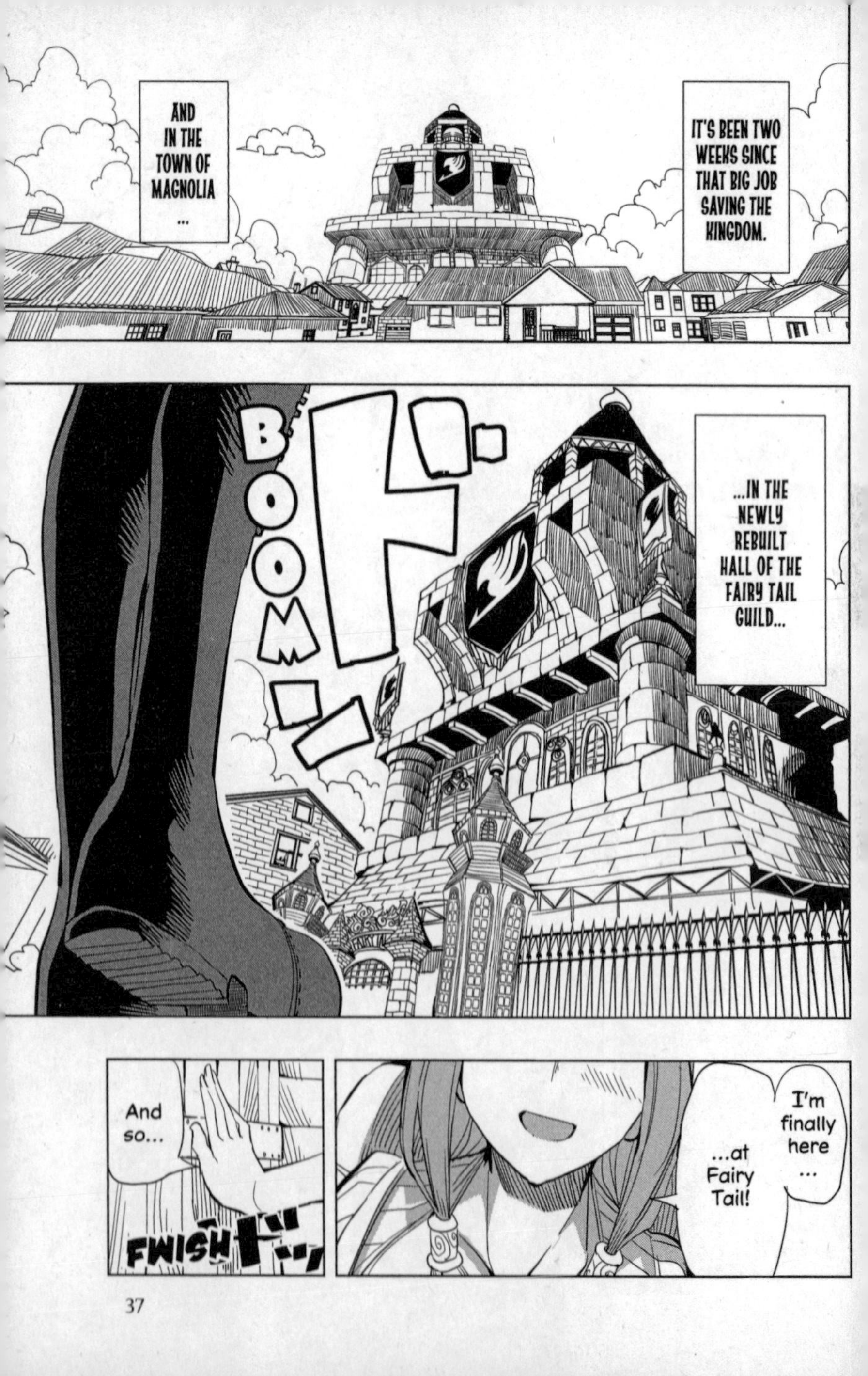
IT'S BEEN TWO WEEKS SINCE THAT BIG JOB SAVING THE KINGDOM.
AND IN THE TOWN OF MAGNOLIA ...
...IN THE NEWLY REBUILT HALL OF THE FAIRY TAIL GUILD...
BOOOM
I'm finally here ...
...at Fairy Tail!
And so...
FWISH

BAM
Natsu, you big jerk!
This time I'm gonna end you!
You wanna fight? I'll give you one!
Good morning, every-one!
TMP TMP
??
Who's that?
Ain't never seen her before.

Nice to meet you all!
HUP
I'm Sumire, and I'm here to be a wizard!
I want to join up with Fairy Tail!
Please make me a member!
MUR-MUR
Oh!
What's this?
Says she wants to join the guild!
MUR-MUR

WHUMPH
I really wanted to meet you!
Wendy-san!
UPH!

Wha-?!
KA-CLICK
Hello, I'm Wendy Marvell.
This girl here...
...says she wants to enter the guild ...

...while giving me a bear hug.
Urng!
Ahem.
THUD

Please forgive me!
I fell in love with Wendy-sempai the minute I saw what she did during the Grand Magic Games!
I wanted to join Fairy Tail so badly, that I came all the way here.
And then when I saw the real Wendy-sempai in person, I couldn't help myself...
SNIFF
SNIFF
Yes, well, we don't do the whole sempai and kohai thing here.
But before any of that, you aren't a member here yet.
And Wendy's not used to being called a sempai, anyway. It'll get her flustered.

You mean I'm...
...a veteran?!
...She's enjoying this?
WHOOSH
What, you like someone, so you want to join? Is that a good enough reason?!
What's wrong with that?
I like having new members! It's a good thing!
It was like that for me at first, too.
You're all taking this very lightly.
So why would you object to it, Carla?
My problem isn't with *her* specifically...
We should just be more cautious when choosing a new member...
Tee hee hee! I know what's wrong with Carla!
?
Mira?

She saw that someone else wants to latch onto Wendy...
...and now she's jealous!
N...
No, I'm not!
What's that hand gesture?
Carla, you're jealous?
Shut up!
GLARE
Eek!
Okay, Master! What do *you* think?!
SNIFF
SNIFF
Hm!
What?! Now me?!
STARE
That's true.
This *is* the kingdom's strongest guild.
It's easy to *say* I want to join, but I'll bet it's going to be ...

... difficult to get in, isn't it?
うる
PLIP
BOING
ぷるん

She's in.
Hey!!
What are you leering at? *That's* what made the decision for you?!
I...
I'm not leering at anything!
You dirty old man!
I'm simply recalling the past.
Fairy Tail was never the type of guild to turn down a prospective member.
You're so obvious!
It's been a while since the master made that face.
AHEM
However...
...since we don't know the extent of your abilities, we cannot send you on a job unsupervised.
Therefore...

I assign Wendy and Carla to be your mentors.
BOOM
You will work with them for a while.
?!
We're mentors ?!
No, hold on, Master!
All right!
Thank you so much, Master!
WHUMP!
Umph!
This time, the master got the hug!
I'm so jeal-ous!
I wonder if I can be a good mentor ...?
...

Then allow me to introduce myself. I'm Wendy, your mentor!
...I'm Carla.
Nice to meet you, sempai!
BAWHOOM
BAWHOOM
From outward appearances, you're far more "advanced."
Don't say that!
What'cha guys doin'?
Ah! Natsu-san!

So you're Natsu-san, the Sala-mander?
Oh, you're the newbie, right?
My name is Sumire. Nice to meet you!
BOW
I heard you're tryin' to be a wizard. What kind of magic do you use?
I SEE!
You're asking me to show you my strength?
Very well. I can do that.
!
SSST
ZLIP
Hey!
There!
That was quick!
TA-DAAH
What is it?
This tree's got limbs!
And very reepy ace.
But you only used a tiny amount of magic!
A good empai *would* otice that!

He's a magic marionette.
Mari-onette?
ZSH
What does that mean?
Heh heh! Showing is faster than explaining.
Move
GRRN
It moves however my magic tells it to.
Oh! That's cool!
WADDLE
WADDLE
Hey, you're more than a wanna-be wizard! You're pretty much a wizard right now!
No. I don't have the control I want.

If I don't focus, this guy goes around ripping off everyone's clothes!
Wha-?!
STRIP
STRIP
...
Oh... Okay.
How about we take this somewhere else?
GONK
VWUMP
Pft! That's hilarious!
Gah!!
Don't you dare look!

AHEM.
Getting our-selves back on track...
Here is the guild's pool.
Wow!
Yo!
It's Wendy and Carla...
...and the new girl!
HEY!
These girls are Cana-san and Lisanna-san.
CZOOM
?
Hey, you!
For a new girl, you've already got a sexy body!
Wait, Cana-san, no!
GRAB
If we're talking about bodies...
ZUUM
?!

I think yours is much sexier, sempai!
ZLOOM
Eek!!
ZLOOM
What are these things wrapping around me?!
Appar-ently, it's Sumire's puppet.
It can give you a nice mas-sage!
How about here?
Does this feel good?
RUB
RUB
RUB
Eek!
E-yaah!
WHUD
In-cred-ible...
You turned lecher-mode Cana into a boneless chicken!
Would anyone else like a try?
We'll pass!
HUFF
HUFF
L-Let's go to the next place.

Oh! It's Gray-san and Juvia-san.
Yo.
Nice to meet you.
I hear that you got some magic way of stripping clothes off of people.
You gotta be careful, or else people will think you're perverted.
You're definitely the last person she wants to hear that from.
This is Levy-san and Lucy-san.
A guided tour of the guild?
Lucy is writing a novel! Do you guys...
...want to read it?
Noo!
And final-ly...

This is the roof area, which also has an observation deck for the guild.

Wow!!

It's the most popular spot for guild members, too.
Someday, Juvia thinks she will bring the one she loves here!
But Gray-sama says no.
The breeze feels so refreshing!
Wow!
So... What do you think of the guild?
It's the best thing ever!
There's so much energy, and everyone's so fun! It's just the best!
Tee hee! That's nice to hear.
When I first came to Fairy Tail, everyone helped me out so much...
...I don't know how helpful I can be, but I'll try to at least do half as much as they did!
Sem-pai...

GWISH
You really are such a grand mentor!
Even though you're tiny.
You didn't need to mention that second part!
If only my body matched ...!
SNIFF
SNIFF
Good going, Wendy!
You're as mature a mentor as anyone here!
Sem-pai...
GASP
Y-Yes?
If the guided tour is over...
...there's a job I was hoping we could do!

A FOREST NEAR MAGNOLIA...
BOOM
There are people dumping garbage in this forest.
Please capture them and correct their behavior.
It's the lowest-class job, at only 10,000 jewels.
I'm surprised you picked something so slight.
I'm still too unsure of myself to go on any high-ranking quests.
Well, you can't let your guard down just because it's a low rank.
You could get lost in the forest, or separated from your party...

TUMP
Let's find these people quick, sempai!
Sumire-san, wait!
TUMP
TUMP
TUMP
TUMP
Separated in no time at all.
YAHOOOOOO!
Wh- What'll we do?
What else can we do but pray this doesn't turn into a disaster?

VWAACH
ドザァァ
That'll do it...
Well!
...Being bad to the bone really gives you a rush, don't it?!
Yaaay!
Ah ha ha!
Illegal Dumping Group Dagaz Gang Reward: 10,000 Jewels
Phew ...
No matter how many times I do it, dirtying such a pristine forest...
...pains me to no end.

That's enough, you bad guys!
Whaa- ?!
THUMP
Who're you?!
I never thought I'd catch the criminals red-handed right at the start of my investiga- tion!
I am rookie Fairy Tail Wizard, Sumire!!
And I refuse to permit you to litter like that!
VWAAM

F-Fairy Tail?!
That's Fiore's strongest guild!
Eek!
What're they here for?!
Just hearing the name scares people!
It really *is* an honor to be among them!
Speaking of which, where is sempai?
Oh, no! She must've gotten lost!
Kh!
Now that's its come to this, I'll just have to arrest them myself!
Prepare your-selves!
MARIONETTE!!
Uwaah!
DWAAH

Punch!
DOKAM
Gaa ...!
...aaa...
...aah?
How'd that feel?!
It... It...

...didn't hurt at all!!
DOKAAM
?!
Oww...
SKRRCH
Humph!
You guys won the Grand Magic Games, so I figured you'd be really strong...
But look at ya!
Yer nothing! Fairy Tail ain't nothing!
Y- You're wrong!
It's... just because I'm really new there ...
The veterans are really amazing!

Shaddap!!
Ow...!!
GANCH
WHAM
First of all, who could respect a guild that lets some useless thing inside their doors anyway?!
This "strongest" rumor's gotta be a lie!
WHAM
Ha ha ha ha!
Ah ha ha ha!
Ha?

BOOOM

Oh!
Gwuh!
DOKAAM
Geh!
BAM
Who are you sup-posed to be...
...er...if you don't mind me asking.
We're with her!
Fairy Tail!
Y-You don't say...
You guys are so different
...

ZWOOOM
Gwaah!!

I know why Wendy-sempai is here...
...but why are the rest of you...?
WAAAH
We heard Sumire was on a quest.
So we all snuck behind you to see what it was about.
Hey! Wake up!
GASP
Eek! Please forgive me!

This is quite a lot of garbage. Was this all you?
Seems like too much.
N-No, it isn't!
This was a request!
We had to be here at this time to dump the trash!
Huh?

A request from who?
D-Dunno.
I met the person at night. Didn't see the face.
It was a woman. And her face had a rose mark.
A rose mark?
Hey, we don't even know if it's garbage in there or not!
What?!
It's too heavy.
So... What *is* in there?
PSSHH

PSSSHHHH
Wha-?!
Some-thing's coming from the barrels?!
Some kind of smoke?!
It's not smoke!
It's...

SLUMP
It's sleeping gas!
Nobody breathe it in...
I-It's too late...
It can't be...
THUD
A... trap...
THUD
What is this? It was supposed to be trash, but it's sleeping gas?
Aah! What is this?!
Oh, shut up!
?!

MARIONETTE WHIP!!
ZWATCH
Gaah!
SPLURCH
M...
Mommy ...
ズルッ
SLUMP

S...
THUD
Su-
mire?
Your
mark...
T-Trap?
But
why
...
ZWAK
?!
ZWIP
?!
I got all
four when
I only
prepped
this trap
for you...
Wendy!

ZLITHER
You were my target all along.
Wendy Marvell!
ZLITHER
From now on, you work for me.
Don't worry. I'll work you to the bone.
?!

Chapter 8: With an Unbreakable Spirit...

Good morning ...
...Wendy-sama!

Wh-Wh-Wh-Wh...
Why are you all dressed like this?!
DAZE
ぼー
Erza-san?
Don't even try.
They are all brain-washed.
?!
BOOM
Sumire-san...?
You've slept for almost ten hours since the forest.
I guess you inhaled too much gas.

So this ...
...sleeping gas was your doing, Sumire-san?
ZUUM
ZWATCH
Eeek!!
RUMBLE
You'd better be more polite than that!
S-Sumire-san?
Because I brought you here as my slave!
Slave ?!
HO HO HO HO!
I-I don't get it!

Grab her.
Yes, Mistress.
GRATCH
Wh- What's wrong with all of you?!
They're just following my orders.
I want you to understand your position.
EH HEH HEH
Wh-What do you intend on doing?!

SCRUB
First, a bath.
SCRUB
SCRUB
Ah ha ha ha!
SCRUB
Wh- What's the bath for?!
Not even slaves should wander around in a filthy condition.
BAWHOOM
Just stay still!
Umph!
Gasp!
I told you, it's futile.
Come on, guys! Wake up!
Okay, next...

Slaves shouldn't have tense bodies, so...
...a massage!
GRIMP
GRIMP
GRIMP
GRIMP
A...
Aaah!

And the spa treatment.
Yes, you're a slave, but if your complexion is off, then it pains those who are forced to see you.
SQUISH
SQUISH
SQUISH
SQUISH
SQUISH
SQUISH
SQUISH
Ahhh...

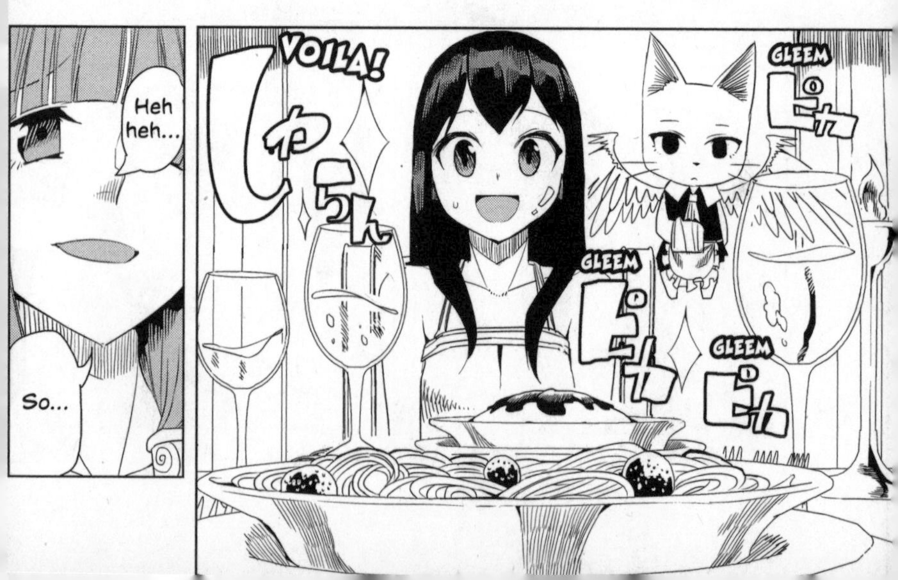
GLEEM
GLEEM
GLEEM
VOILA!
Heh heh...
So...

VWAAM
Do you understand your position now?
...I've never been treated better.
Please eat up before it gets cold!
Y-Yes, Ma'am!
What is going on here...?
A person comes to the guild, eager to please...
...then she targets me...
...and sort of kidnaps me...
...making everybody act all weird.
NOM
STARE
Where is this place?
What are you after?
...
SHKK
Well, she'll find out soon enough.
So why not tell her...
?!

BOOM
...what it is we're after.
When did they get here?
Let me introduce you...
We're the dark guild, Rose Marionette.
And this is our base.
Dark Guild
Rose Marionette

What would a dark guild want with me?
Not revenge, right?
I don't remember doing anything to you.
Revenge? Don't be ridiculous.
All we want is your dragon slayer magic.
Dragon slayer magic?
Yes...
Dragon slayer magic. A magic intended to kill beasts as powerful as dragons!
The power you showed at the Grand Magic Games was more than we could've imagined!
And we think it's a waste for all that power to go to just a few people.
That's when we got an idea.
We could study a dragon slayer...
ZUUM
...and figure out a way for anyone to use those powers.

CATCHER
B
And we can do that...
...with this magic-absorbing device!
BAAM
GRATCH
VWIRL
?!
VWUM
VWUM
Huh?
What is...?
ZLURP
ZLURP
Huh? Wait a second!
What is this?
Begin!
CLANG

ZLOOSH
Eyaah!

BLUP
BLUP
BLUP
BLUP
SHIIING
I think ...
...my magic's getting sucked out of me...
I've felt this before ...
You re-member now?

It's from the resort where you all went to have fun, but got captured by a dark guild...
We've made this device ten times more effective than the one they had.
!!
Why would you guys...
Why else?
We're the ones who gave our device to dark guilds all over Fiore.
It's to gather data!
You people are...
FSHHHHH
?!
Oh!
It's all finished!
KATUNK
ROLL

KA-CLUNK
What is this?!
It came out of that magic-sucking machine!
Now that's top-grade stuff!
GRIMP
Why wait? Let's give it a try!
A try? Try what?!
SST
The ball's stuffed full of your dragon slayer magic!
Hi-yah!
I just throw it, and...
WHOOSH

KABOOM

As you can see...
...it becomes an immensely powerful magic bomb.
Now, all we gotta do is sell them to every dark guild in the country.
I think 10,000 jewels per ball is about right.
It'll take dark guilds into a brand-new era.
One that'll make us the richest people on the continent!
No...
FLASH
I won't let you!

GRATCH
Oww!
Come on, guys!
Never disrespect the mistress!
Heh heh...
It seems she's suffering from my magic. Uho!
?!
The moment you see this pendulum, it's all over.
It means you're under my hypnotic spell!
They answer to no one but me. Uho!
Rose Marionette
Hypnotic Gorilla

So...
...just sit back, relax, and let us suck your power away...
ZLURP
ZLURP
Oww!
...for-ever.
Su-mire... san...

Even the strongest wizards can only last three hours before passing out...
So my question is...
...how did you manage to last for seventeen whole hours?
BOOM
HUFF
HUFF
HUFF
It's not unusual for wizards to die after the second or third extraction.
But, I guess even you have your limits.
Let's stop here for now.
PACHIK
HUFF
HUFF
Why do you do things like this...
Su-mire-san?
WOBBLE
HUFF
HUFF
...?
Didn't I already tell you?
We need the money.
I want as much as I can get.

Fairy Tail's nothing more than a stepping stone to that goal.
!
They say you're Fiore's strong-est...
...but you never saw through my lie.
So your guild isn't all it's cut out to be.
You're wrong.
You didn't fool anyone...
Huh?
I mean ...
...when you came to the guild, Sumire-san...
...you were having a good time. That was from the heart!
GLARE
Sumire-san...
...you think Fairy Tail is actually ...
GSHK
Shut up!

You don't know anything!
You're just a slave!
You *still* think you're my mentor?!
The entire reason I tried to attach my-self to you was...
...because you seemed to be the easiest of the dragon slayers to trick!
But even so, you're a pain.
Here you think you can "believe" in me after what I've put you through?
There's only one thing you can trust in this world, and that's money!
If it's for money, I'm willing to work with scum—like these guys in this guild!
If I save up the money from these bombs ...
...then this awful life...

You got a problem with this life?
You can always quit, you know?
As you wish...
ZLURCH

KOFF

SHIVER
Huh?
Wh...
Why...?
THUD
VACH
It was nothing personal.
I just never thought of you as one of us.
And once you had the dragon slayer captured, your usefulness was at an end.
We were only using you.

We gotta protect our secrets. When a pawn's use is fulfilled, it's eliminated.
That's the unwritten law of Rose Marionette.
Don't give me that crap...
HUFF
HUFF
I can't...
...let myself die now!
I still...
...have things that I must do...
Good work.
Time to go.

DWOHH

No way!
How can she even move?!
Hya-aah!
B-BOOM

CURING MAGIC!
GLOW
Just stay still...
...
Wendy-san...
Why?
I betrayed you and your friends...
...
!
Everyone makes mistakes.
?!

And correcting the mistakes of a kohai...
...is the job of a mentor.
HUFF
HUFF
She can't be serious ...
Does she really think she can fight all of us in that condition?!

Chapter 9:
Light that Pierces the Depths of the Heart

Now come along quietly...
... Wendy Marvell ...
KA-SHIIING
Wendy ...
I gotta admire the guts it takes to attack when you're so outnum-bered!

ZLASSH
But you're too slow!
Guh!
Gak ...
THUD
My blade is even faster than Titania's!
Even if we didn't hypnotize her, you guys would *still* lose!
HUFF
HUFF
Some-one like you...
...wouldn't last against Erza if she really went at it...!
Yes, about Erza...

She's enjoying a nice little tea party over here.
I must say, this Earl Grey is excellent.
SIP
SIP
You guys?!
They're under the illusion that they're at some enjoyable tea party thanks to my hypnotic spell! Uho!
N-No way...
Let's just stop there.
You see how this will turn out, right?
And if things go too far, you'll die, and we'll lose the money for our bombs!
But if you go along with it, we'll guarantee their safety.
And what about Sumire?

Can't change that.
She knows the guild's secrets.
Then no thanks!
I don't think you get your position.
You're on the verge of death.
And your friends will be held as hostages.
Even so...
...I refuse.
GRIMP

If I sell one person to save my friends...
...no Fairy Tail wizard would thank me for that!
You will never get your hands on Sumire-san!
Then we have no choice.
We're just going to have to cut off your arms and legs so you can't resist anymore.
And it's your own fault for not listening to reason!
Urk!
ZLIP
What'll I do?!
If only I could manage to let the others get away...

VWIRL
?!
That's far enough!
GRATCH
?!
Sumire-san?
Please don't move.
You guys, too!
If any of you move, Wendy Marvell's dead.
You little ...!
What are you thinking?!
My goals haven't changed.

I want all the cash I'm owed in this, and guarantees that I won't be harmed!
Once I have that, you can have Wendy!
No, that's not enough!
Haul out all the money you have right now!
After I get it, you can boil her, bake her, whatever you want!
S-Sumire-san...
Hey, thanks for saving me, Wendy-san.
But it looks like I need the money after all.

Pft!
Ah ha ha ha ha!
I was wondering what you'd say!
After looking down on us...
Here you are, bad to the bone–a true Dark Guild member after all!
Okay, sure...
We'll give you everything we've made so far.
We'll get it back and more after selling a few bombs.
There!
WHOOSH

Just kidding!
You were so dis-tracted by the money ...
...you failed to notice your back was completely unguard-ed!
GRATCH
!!
Hyah!
DOKAAM
Aah!

Ow
...
ドサッ
WHUD
スキャーッ
SKRRCH
Kh!

Ah
ha
ha
ha
ha!
You
really
are
pathetic!
A failure
as a
wizard
and a
human!
Well,
what do
you
expect?

Everybody
wants
something.
And if you
wave it in front
of them, you'll
get an opening
to attack!
Uho!
You
did just
what I
wanted.
I finally
managed to
get you far
enough away
from them...
From
my
guild
sempai.
Uho?

Uho-ooo!
ZWATCH

What? We were attacked from behind?
By Sumire's puppets?!
But too bad for you! You missed!
No...

We're split in two. Us...

...and Fairy Tail.

...Hey, go get them!
We can't let them run!
GWAR
I won't let you!
Uwah!
WHOOSH

Wendy-san, get out of here!
Take everybody and go!
Now!
Sumire-san...
Then... that was on purpose?
It'll take all my power just to hold these four off!
So, go! Now!
Hold us off?
You're gravely mistaken.
?!

THUD
Gah!
Sumire-san!

A pathetic power like yours can't hold one of us off, let alone four!
But you did surprise me.
I thought money was all you wanted.
You came here willing to ignore morals for a profit, right?
So what could get you to try protecting someone now?
HUFF
HUFF
I haven't ...
I haven't changed my mind. Money is the main thing...
You're kidding!
Why?! What would make you go so far just for money?!
I can't help it!

I need money...
...if I want to be able to live with my kids.

What?
Kids...?
Sumire-san, you had kids this whole time?!
They're not *my* kids...

They're the kids at my church!
Church?!
There's a small rural church about a two-day walk from here.
They're desperately poor and struggling to survive, but they're managing by helping each other.

Even the church is having money problems ...
...and they'll be forced to shut down without more money!
But I...
...I never wanted to leave everyone at the church. Even if I had to starve to death...
Everyone felt that way!
After all...
...you see Fairy Tail as your family, right?
Well, because that run-down church was a priceless place for me...
...!
...I decided to do business with a dark guild...
...It seemed like the most efficient way to get money with my magic.
No way...
Then why are you trying to rescue me now...?!
You still need money to help keep your family alive, right?
...

Wendy-san, I've opened my eyes thanks to you!
I don't think anyone in my family would have been happy...
...if I saved them with the dirty money I got through evil acts!
I don't know why I didn't think of it before...
...
Sumire-san...
GRIT
Now!
It isn't too late!
Get everyone out of here while I hold them off!
I-I can't!
I can't run away leaving you behind!

!!
How *long* is this conversation supposed to be?!
VWOOH
Are you done with your boring chat?
Just listening wore me out!
HUP
So let's get this over with.
...!
I won't let you!
VOOSH

You might be Fairy Tail...
VWOOSH

But you're out of power!
ZWAMM

GHK
HUFF
HUFF
N-Not yet...
SHK
SHK
SHK

Aaah!
It'd be a hassle if you started getting worked up again.
So I might as well make it so you can never move again!
GHK
Wait...
Don't... lay a finger... on my mentor!
You should worry about yourself!
GACK
Guh!
You betrayed her, yet you call her your men-tor?
That's pretty brazen, even for us! Uho!
Since you're going to die now. Uho.
Maybe he's absolutely right.
If this is my punish-ment, I'll take it...
...My only wish...
...is to at least spare her!
No...!

DOGOOM

Gah...

Phew!

Glad I made it in time.
But it indicates my training is insufficient.
TWITCH
TWITCH
Huh?
Erza-san?!
Y-You couldn't have broken the hypnotic spell! Uho!
That wouldn't be possible! Uho!
No one has ever broken my hypnotic spell before...

GAWHAAAM
So that was you?!
Gah!
My right eye is artificial...
...so hypnotic power only affects me halfway.
And now ...
S- Stay back!
You won't like what I'll do to her if you move!
VWAP

Guh!
DOGAAM
SKRRCH
Kh!
Now I see!
The minute the hypnotic wizard was taken out, it broke the spell, huh?
Are you okay, Wendy?
Lucy-san! Juvia-san!
We'll discuss this later.
VWOOM
Though I have many questions.
VWOOM

You bore it well.
We'll handle the rest.

KA-SHNG

I think this is perfect!
I've wanted to fight you ever since I saw you in the Grand Magic Games, Erza Scarlet!
I'm Lauren, of Rose Marionette!

We'll face off and find out who the best swords-woman in the kingdom is!
ZWAT
Huh?!
EYAAAH!!
Sorry, but...
...none of the sword fighters in the Games were as weak as you.
D-Don't be scared of them!
We were able to capture them before!
Attack them all at once!

Geh!
DOKAAM!!
Guoh!
GAWHAM
They're so damn strong!
Even though they totally fell for Sumire's trick?!
That's true.
But if you people hadn't tried to hurt her...
...this might not have been your fate!
You should've taken care of your comrades!
But it's too late for you now!

AFTER IT WAS ALL OVER...
...THE FIRST THING THAT SUMIRE-SAN DID...
...WAS FORMALLY APOLOGIZE TO US.
All right. I've heard your whole story now. Ultimately, you tried to save us, right?
Exactly! Everybody can make a mistake!
So let's all go back!
To Fairy Tail!
Sem-pai...

Forgive me, but...
...I can't go back with you.
What ?!

Why not?!
I don't think someone with a sinful past like me belongs in Fairy Tail.

Don't worry!
The wording is harsh, but it's true.
There are plenty of criminal-like folks!
GLOOM
Most importantly, I hurt Wendy, and she's the same age as some of the kids at church...
I know our money troubles made me a little crazy, but I can't forgive myself...
Sumire-san...

I don't even know if I can face them like this...
SSST
...so I'll try to atone for the crimes I've committed...
...while attempting to come up with a way for everyone in that church to keep living together.
If I manage to get it all worked out...
...I'm hoping then, maybe you'd be willing to mentor me one more time...?
I will!
AND AFTER THAT, WE PARTED WAYS WITH SUMIRE.

Are you sure about this...
... Wendy?
Yeah. I'm sure that some-day...
...she'll come back to Fairy Tail.
SEVERAL DAYS LATER...
...A LARGE LOAD OF PRESENTS WAS DELIVERED TO A PARTICULAR CHURCH, WAY OUT IN THE COUNTRY.
So we have to work to make it an even better guild for Sumire's return!
I suppose so...
RUMOR HAS IT THAT THE RETURN ADDRESS ON THE PACKAGES READ, "FAIRY TAIL."
AND ARRIVING BACK AT THE GUILD...
CLAMOR
You ain't gettin' away with that!
Took the words right outta my mouth!
CLAMOR
They're fighting again?!
I don't know if the building will last until Sumire-san gets back here!

Chapter 10: The Ultimate Girl Power

WHAA-?!
Number 3
Erza Scarlet
Number 1
Lucy Heartfilia
Number 2
Wendy Marvell

Number 4 (tie)
Mavis Vermillion
Number 4 (tie)
Mirajane Strauss
Number 6
Juvia Lockser
I NEVER THOUGHT I'D CLAIM FIRST PLACE!
I-I DON'T BELIEVE IT!
OR GET THE FIVE-HUNDRED-GRAND-JEWEL PRIZE!
YAY!
VWUMP
THANK YOU ALL!
I'M SOOO HAPPY!
I'LL OBVIOUSLY USE THIS TO PAY MY RENT!

...And that was...
...the dream I had.
GONG
What a wonderful dream!
What could make you depressed after that?!

When I realized the five-hundred grand was a dream...
...it only made me more conscious of how poor I am right now...
I can't pay rent...
My living expenses are in-sufficient ...
Lucy-san...
Okay, putting that aside, why were Cana and I called here today?
Well, about that...

Since the weather's so nice...
...we thought we'd clean up Fairy Hills!
And we're a little short-handed, so...
...help us out!
Aw.
I was planning on going shopping after this.
Shop-ping?
Is shopping your *real* motiva-tion?
Huh?
I happened to have seen you a little while back in the shopping district...
TWITCH
After you just told us you probably couldn't afford rent?
Window shop-ping!

...getting free bread crusts from the baker...
Nooo!
Sorry, I didn't say any-thing...
But it's hard to say hi in that situation...
はっはっはー
HAHAHA
Lucy...
Y-You got it wrong !!
You see, I just happened to have a craving for bread crust that day...
...but nobody was selling them...
Come to think of it, Lu-chan...
...I saw you in the food market spending your lunch time at the free sample tables...
You saw that?!
And I witnessed Lucy attacking other customers for clothing on sale for a limited time only.
And I...
Please make it stop!

GRGLGRGLGRGL
SST
Assist us with the clean-ing.
We shall pay for your time.
With a meal as well.
I love a good cleaning.
I can't stop thinking about it though.
SPLETCH

If we actually had a Miss Fairy Girl contest...
...who do you think would win?
Oh, come on, Cana!
Well... I doubt it'd turn out like my dream...
...where I got number one.
But there's Mira-san and Erza and Cana...
And you're cute too, Levy!
...
I don't know about that.
Personally, I'd vote for Lucy.
Oh! You think so, too, Erza?
Huh?
Where'd *that* come from?!
Such contests revolve around one's feminine charms.
In other words, "girlish power."
I would prevail in a test of swords...
...however, I might fail in girlish power. I must be more diligent.
I don't know about that...

I think so, too!
Lucy-san, you're so pretty and nice!
Huh?
You have even posed for *Weekly Sorcerer.*
Well, you've always had good assets, so.
Huh?!
Hey, Miss Popular!
S-Stop that, you guys!
Flattery won't get you anything, you know!
Ha ha ha!
And you're really cute in the way that you eat your lunch at the free-sample counter!
Waaah!!
Cana... What'd I tell you?!

Lu-chan's gone bye-bye.
Cana is to blame.
O-Okay, sorry!
Um...
Didn't I say you had great assets?
And a lot of guild guys have a crush on you!
With a little polish, you could have your pick!
... Really?

You could even have one of those cool-acting guys like ***Gray!***
You might knock 'em dead!
What!
Hey! Gray is the ***last*** thing you should talk about!
I mean, what if Juvia were to hear?
Not a problem!
Juvia's far away on a job.

Who wants to seduce Gray-sama?
Eeek!
J-Juvia ?!
I finished the job quickly, so I'm back.
RUMBLE
Juvia never thought she'd see a stray thief here!
I-I am not!
She isn't doing anything, Juvia!
I was just talking about Lucy's girlish power!
Girlish power ?
That's right!
I was just saying that Lucy had a high level of girlish power.
Is that so...?
Yes, Juvia concurs that Lucy has girlish power.
And were she to train up, those powers might grow even stronger.
Y-You think so? Thank you!

AND NOW YOU'RE GOING TO STEAL GRAY-SAMA WHEN I'M NOT LOOKING?!
Because Gray-sama is the coolest man in the world!
What are you even talking about?!
Why is that always your conclusion?!
Who knew an enemy in love would hit so close to home...
...Juvia is left with no other choice!
Lucy! Juvia challenges you to a contest of girlish power!
And the loser must remove all claims to Gray-sama!!
Huh?!
BAM

A contest of girlish power? What does that even mean?
Heh!
This sounds like fun!
Huh?
I hereby declare the Girlish Power Contest featuring Lucy vs. Juvia!
And it starts now!
I accept your chal-lenge!
Huh?!
What are you talking about, Cana?!
The Girlish Power Contest! What else?

Juvia, who is determined to prove her love for Gray...
...and her rival in love, Lucy! Pitted against each other!
Now just hold on, Cana!
And all five of us will be judges!
What's that?
Let's just put Juvia's fears to rest and get back to cleaning!
Quit starting weird stuff!
What can you say that Juvia would believe?
The best way to calm her is to let her do what she wants.
But ...
FUME FUME
A girlish contest...?
Sounds fascinat-ing.
Well, if everyone's so worked up...
Stop it!

HEHE HEHE
No worries!
You can trust my judgment!
BOOZE
YEAH
There is no judgment more impaired than hers!
Fine.
I guess I'll go along with this for a bit.
Then let the contest begin!
First, for you two...
BOOOM
...A cleaning competition in Levy's room!

My room?!
Cleaning competi-tion?!
HEH!
It's fun-damental for a lady to always keep her space tidy.

For the purposes of this challenge...
...I've pushed over all of Levy's stacks of books!
VWAAM
What a rotten thing to do, Cana!
We'll split the room in two with a curtain...
SKRRT
And the two of you have to straighten it up within the time limit!
The judges will determine who won.
We're considering this a run-through for when you invite your lover to your room.
Ready? Start!
Here Juvia goes!
Honestly...
I only came here because they promised me dinner after we clean, so why am I doing this?
Well, whatever. Let's just get this over with.

Okay!
Done!
That was quick! And thorough!
That's Lucy for you!
She displays incredible girlish power, right off the bat!
It's because I live on my own.
But I don't think it has much to do with being girlish though.
Juvia is finished, too!
Oh?! Juvia's pretty fast, too!
We'll just open the curtain...
...and reveal if Juvia is any match for Lucy's skills...!
FWISH

Um...
What is this?
HEH HEH
Juvia was a little unsatisfied with *just* cleaning.
It was then that Juvia noticed ...
...there was no Gray-sama!
How can you call a room perfect with no Gray-sama in it?!

I vote for Lucy!
LUCY WINS THE ROUND.
Why?!
You get points counted against you for decorations that don't take other people's interests into account.
That and you can't bring a boyfriend in here.
Besides, with that many Gray photos, you seem like a total stalker.
And where'd you get them anyway?
You don't understand the value of Gray-sama...
...Juvia doesn't approve of the level of judging!
ARGH!
Not quite what this contest is about though...
But boy am I glad this is all over!
Not that I want to win Gray.
Over? Who said anything is over?

Now we enter round two!
Round two?!
You mean it's not over?!
Hm?
We're doing best three out of five, right?
Three out of five?!
Juvia wants round two!
See? Juvia is prepared.
And the theme is...
Well, I'm not interested!

BOOM
A cooking competition!

As they say, the way to a man's heart is through his stomach ...
...and we know that guys can't resist a good cook!
This contest to test your cooking skills was inevitable!
You're right!
It's a classic, all right.
JUDGE

KATUNK
Umph!
That was quick!
Both finished their dishes at the same time!
What could they have made in such a short time?!
Reveal your dishes!

BOOM
Lucy made pasta!
B-BOOM
And Juvia made a cup of tea!
Um...
Tea?
Yes.

It's Earl Grey tea!
And any dish with Gray-sama in it is bound to beat pasta!
Steeping is not cooking, so...
And it doesn't actually have Gray in it.
LUCY VS. JUVIA
2 WINS
0 WINS

SSSIP

Lu-chan, you're already at two wins!
The next match could decide it.
Pasta and tea is a surprisingly good combination.
When did you become such engaged viewers?!
Now for the next round!

Round three!
The Sexy Pose Competition!

Showing off your assets is a basic trait of girlish power!
We will be judging how you two do striking the same poses!
I never thought I'd wear a swim suit in Fairy Hills!
GLANCE
But whatever. Let's get this over with!
Right, Juvia?
IF JUVIA LOSES THIS, JUVIA LOSES GRAY-SAMA FOREVER!
PANIC
PANIC
PANIC
She's in full-on depression mode.
It's a mis-understand-ing, but she won't even listen to me.
Which means that Gray is the only thing on her mind, I guess.
I kinda feel sorry for her.
HMM
Maybe I should let her win this one.

And will *you* be okay with that?
?!
Erza-san?
You're not thinking about throwing the round on purpose, are you?
The only reason Juvia has been competing so hard...
...is out of respect and fear for your true girlish power.
And you would consider...
...betraying that sense of competition?
You're really going to run away?
I... suppose not.

All right. I'll take on Juvia for real.
Throwing a fight isn't the Fairy Tail way.
?
So watch closely, Juvia!
The pose of a *Weekly Sorcerer* pinup veteran!
WHOOSH
Watch my girlish power!

Oh!
Ooh!
FLASH
FLASH
FLASH
Fantastic, Lucy-san!
You're glowing!
KACHIK
KACHIK
Calm yourself, Wendy!
Lucy's really giving it her all! Now you have to go all out, Juvia!
Me? Go "all out"?
After shedding all her inhibitions, Lucy becomes the very essence of girlish power!
And the only way to win this round is to find some pose that can overwhelm this classic!!
O-Over-whelm *that?!*
How can Juvia do that?!

J...
Juvia is too shy for this...
But since this is for Gray-sama...
...Juvia can handle this!

This is definitely a win for Juvia.
Wait a miniute!
She even made my heart leap for a second.
LUCY VS. JUVIA
2 WINS
1 WINS
What kind of judgment is that after telling me to take on Juvia for real?!
Forgive me, Lucy.
However, you have forgotten something crucial.
The purity of shy innocence.
Don't treat me like some nympho!
I don't accept this...!
Next we have the First Date Costume Competition !!

Ohh!
TA-DAH
Well, we have a daring costume here!
A bust line to blow their minds!
A skirt revealing those supple thighs!
Yes, a costume set for high impact and maximum exposure!
...
But it's not something you'd wear on a first date, is it?
What's with the cat ears?
Whaa?!
SHOCK
Aren't you supposed to look cute for your first date?
Observe.
Cast your eyes upon Juvia over there.

A white dress that indicates purity.
TA-DA
A dress that isn't too showy, but defines the body's contours well. A subtle sexiness.
This is truly a costume fit for a first date.
I hope Gray-sama gets here soon!
And note the perfect performance of a maiden waiting.
Juvia-san, you're so cute!
Gray-sama! Juvia did it!
We give Juvia the win!
Oh, come on!
LUCY VS. JUVIA
2 WINS 2 WINS

The next will not only break the tie, but decide...
...which girl has more girlish power!
!!
Lucy-san?
What's wrong?
N-No, nothing.
What's happened to me?
At first, this was just a pain!
But now, I don't want to lose!
Invisible sparks are flying between them.
Lucy's finally bringing her A-game!
Yes.
VZZT
Now with the mood just right, and everyone ready to battle...
...we bring you to the final event!
Hello!

Is Juvia here?
Mira-san?
What's wrong?
I have a message for Juvia.
Juvia is just about to enter the final round of a competition with Lucy.
Sorry, but your message will have to wait.
Really?
If I have to.
Gray was asking for Juvia to come see him...
TWITCH
He said he has a job, and Juvia would be the perfect partner to work with.
Now!
Juvia, time for the match!

GRAY-SAMA CALLED FOR ME?!
NOT ONLY THAT, BUT TO WORK HAND-IN-HAND?!
WHAM
Gray-sama! Juvia is on her way to you!
YAHOOOOOO!
いやっほおおお
THUMP

...Why don't we simply... finish cleaning?
Good idea.
Mmm...

So many things kept us busy today.
Thanks for all your help.
But in the end, we never learned who was the more girlish one, right Lu-chan?
Yeah, I don't care about that.
Hm?
In the end, wasn't it you who cared the most?
Huh?
No! Not at all!
But ...
...are you gonna tell me what it was?
Huh?

The theme of the final competi-tion?
Oh?
You really *are* cute!
GRAB
Eyaaah!

SQUEEZE
I was thinking of a bust comparison!
Hey!
Stop that, Cana...!
SQUEEZE
SQUEEZE
SQUEEZE

Well yours feel nice!
But are you bigger than Juvia?
FWUMP
FWUMP
Don't know! Don't care!
And I want it to stop!

Hey, you all!
RATTLE
When you're done with your baths, come to the dining hall.
Dinner's already made!
Dinner!

MUNCH
MUNCH
This is great!
That's Mira for you!
There's enough for seconds.
This is just my way of showing appreciation...
...for your hard cleaning!
...
Now *that* is girlish power!
The real deal was here all along.
?
A long time ago, she was hopeless though.
Did you say something?
No. Nothing.

FAIRY GIRLS
vol.2········END

THANK YOU FOR PICKING THIS UP!

BONUS MANGA
THE ROAD HOME FROM CHAPTER 6
I'm kind of sick of card games...
So let's each show off a talent!
BOOM
Show off a talent?
I heard it's what people do while vacationing.
It'll help everyone get to know each other better.
I see.
When you say, "show off a talent," do you mean something like this?
Heh heh
See? My thumbs come off!

Y-Yes...
That's so... interesting.
Yes. Um. Fascinating.
はぁーー
SIGH
What's with the totally bored look?!
I was only doing it to be supportive!
GLOOM
Don't cry, Lucy. That only makes you even *more* pathetic.
I'm amazed!
You can amputate your thumb and reattach it!
Wendy, you're sweet when you're gullible.
At the risk of being presumptuous, I could give an example.
You have a special talent?
What is it?!

Ta-dah!
Now she's got horns coming out of her head!
PFT!
Wh-Wh-Wh-What's that sup-posed to be?
SHOOM
The first master is sticking her hands through Erza's body!
SHOOM
Well I *am* a ghost, you know.
So *that's* a talent?!
See?
Now my hands are going through her eyes!
Eek!
AND THIS CONTINUED UNTIL WE FINALLY ARRIVED AT OUR STATION.

SUMIRE'S STORY AFTER CHAPTER 10
Hello everyone at Fairy Tail!
This is Sumire.
I'm now on a journey to try to atone for the things I did as a dark guild member.
All the presents you sent to the kids at the church brought smiles to their faces.
I can't even begin to thank you!
But as a token, I'm sending pictures of all the kids.
I hope they get to you safely.
SEVERAL DAYS LATER...
HEY!
Maybe it's a reply from Wendy and Fairy Tail!

Just a letter?
Oh! Here are pictures!
...
What's being done to them?!
THIS LEFT SUMIRE CONFUSED.
You can stop taking pictures now!
HEH
I can sell 'em for 500 jewels a piece!
No, don't!

Translation Notes:

Japanese is a tricky language for most Westerners, and translation is often more art than science. For your edification and reading pleasure, here are notes on some of the places where we could have gone in a different direction with our translation of the work, or where a Japanese cultural reference is used.

Page 35, Host Club

For a long time in Japan, men could go to "hostess clubs" where customers would pay to converse with the young hostesses, who would pour somewhat overpriced drinks and cater to their client. There are now "host clubs" where women can have the same service from handsome young men.

Page 41 Sempai

Although we've used the words "mentor" and "veteran" often in this translation, the Japanese word for this is *sempai.* Its counterpart is *kohai.* This is a bit more generalized a relationship than mentor/ protégé since anyone in an organization (sports team, club, school, business) who has been in the organization longer can be consider a *sempai,* and anyone who has been in for less time can be considered a *kohai.*

Page 58, Jewels

In most fantasy, the currency used in the fantasy world is intuitively equivalent to the currency used by the intended reader. So if, for example, a horse in a fantasy universe written for American audiences costs four-hundred silver pieces, then the reader can automatically assume that the horse costs something around $400 USD. The same is true for *Fairy Tail*, but only with "jewels" being equivalent to "yen." And a quick-and-dirty conversion for yen is 100 yen to 1 US dollar. So 10,000 jewels would be about $100 USD.

Fairy Girls volume 2 is a work of fiction. Names, characters, places, and incidents are the products of the author's imagination or are used fictitiously. Any resemblance to actual events, locales, or persons, living or dead, is entirely coincidental.

A Kodansha Comics Trade Paperback Original.

Published in the United States by Kodansha Comics, an imprint of Kodansha USA Publishing, LLC, New York.

Publication rights for this English edition arranged through Kodansha Ltd., Tokyo.

First published in Japan in 2015 by Kodansha Ltd., Tokyo
ISBN 978-1-63236-317-6

Printed in the United States of America.

www.kodanshacomics.com

9 8 7 6 5 4 3 2 1

Translation: William Flanagan
Lettering: AndWorld Design
Editing: Haruko Hashimoto
Kodansha Comics edition cover design by Phil Balsman